Introduction

One of the most nerve-wracking experiences in the police recruitment process is the oral board interview. This is due to what many consider the subjective nature of all panel interviews, whether it is an assessment center or oral board. Nonetheless, it is the go to procedure for many agencies around the country, and will be for the foreseeable future. Agencies favor the oral board as a major factor in hiring due to the fact that they can have representatives from the community, local government, and police officers on the board. This allows the community to take part in the screening process for new officers and in turn, hopefully, will limit liability in the future.

The scenarios presented in this book are taken from law enforcement officials around the country, as well as questions that I have personally answered during oral board interviews. Having twenty years on one of the largest police departments in the country, I decided it was time to move to another part of the United States, somewhere a little more scenic. I was able to do very well on the oral boards for multiple new agencies. I received extremely positive feedback from the board members and recruiters involved in the process concerning my performance on the oral boards. This, in turn, led to top rankings on eligibility lists. I realized, however, that without my prior experience to fall back on, I would have been caught completely off guard by the types of questions that are asked in these oral boards. I hope that this book will provide you with a more thorough synopsis of the oral board process, as well as a look into the types of scenarios that will be presented to you.

The most important aspect of any oral board will be your pre-interview mental preparation. It is very important that you realize that the oral board is not there to break you down or demean you in any way. The job of the board is to determine if the candidate will make a good Police Officer. More importantly, does this candidate have the strong moral and ethical compass that is needed from a Police Officer in a modern law enforcement environment? They will also attempt to determine if you, the candidate, have the intestinal fortitude to put your hands on a criminal and fight them until you have them in custody. Or, on an even higher level, do you have the mental toughness to pull the trigger in a deadly force situation? The questions are designed to try and determine if you, the candidate, can "flip that switch" from a compassionate police officer working school patrol one day, to someone who may be forced to take the life of a dangerous individual the next day.

The scenarios are designed to gauge your responses in several areas, primarily ethics, problem solving, and communications. Ethics will always be the first and foremost issue to be addressed. It has been my experience that the most damage to a police department comes from police officers that cross the line into criminal or immoral activity. This is something that weakens a department and brings unnecessary pain and risk to the hard working officers who are doing their job correctly. When responding to the scenarios, do not let the fact that someone is wearing a badge give them a free pass. It is important that the board realizes that you are a person above reproach who will not be intimated from doing your job in the correct manner.

Many scenarios will put you in the role of an officer attempting to solve a problem for the community. Patience is the key to these scenarios. Allow the board to complete the scenario, they often add extra drama to the scenario by role-playing, and then calm the table down. Let your best judgment and common sense guide you during these scenarios. The board will not be looking for exact police procedure from a new hire, but they are looking for the ability to project and be a forward thinker. Allow your answer to expand by drawing in the community, local government agencies, and any other resource you may need to solve the problem. What they do not want to hear is that you, as a patrol officer, would not be able to handle the situation. Do not let the board get the impression that a community issue is something that is "above your pay grade." Be decisive and assume that you will be provided the resources you need to tackle the issue.

Remember, the board will not ever tell you that you are right or wrong on any question. You will only note them scribbling furiously while you give your answer. Do not let this silence create any doubt in your mind while you are giving your response. Remain confident in your answer and do not allow the board to change your mind mid-answer with a challenge question. This is a common tactic to throw the candidate off kilter and determine if the future officer will allow himself or herself to be swayed when handling a situation.

Most importantly, remain calm. If you allow your good judgment, your strong ethics, and communication skills to take the lead, you will ace the oral boards. Remember that the board is not there to eliminate you from contention as a candidate; they are there to find the best candidate for their police department. They want the candidate that can represent their city on the street and do the job in a professional manner. Make yourself the candidate that stands out from the crowd!

Good luck,

Sgt. C. R. Reyna

Public Interaction – Scenario #1

Scenario: You are invited to an elementary school to speak to a group of parents. They are telling you that the high school students are speeding down the main road, through the school zone, and endangering the kids. The parents are upset and want answers as to what the police are going to do about it. How would you handle this situation?

Sample answer: *First, I would tell the parents that I understand their concerns, and that the safety of their children is the number one priority. I would explain to the parents that I am going to personally survey the location and see if there are additional safety measures that could be put in place to slow down the traffic in the area. These measures could include school zone signs, flashing lights to indicate the school zone, or even the possibility of speed bumps being placed in the road. I would then contact the correct agencies to assist me in having these safety measures put in place if needed. I would also assure the parents that I, or another officer, will be out there to monitor the traffic and enforce a zero tolerance policy for any and all school zone violations until the additional safety measures are available. I would then give the parents my departmental contact information so that any future issues can be addressed.*

Notes: This scenario requires patience before you answer. It is important that you allow the board to completely explain the scenario to you before you attempt to answer the group. There may be additional information that the board adds as you begin to answer, so be prepared to stop, take in the new information, and continue with your response. This scenario is designed to gauge your response in dealing with public safety issues. What may be a huge safety issue to others may not seem that important to you. However, a large part of police work is being able to bridge that gap and empathize with the concerns of others.

Use of Force – Scenario #2

Scenario: You respond to a call in which another officer is asking for assistance. When you arrive, the officer is engaged in a physical altercation with the suspect. The suspect does not have weapons of any type, and he and the other officer are in close physical contact. How would you respond to this situation?

Sample answer: *I would immediately come to the assistance of my fellow officer. Since the suspect is not armed, and considering that the other officer is in close physical contact with the suspect, I would go "hands on" with the suspect. I would then use the amount of force necessary to make the arrest. I would refrain from using a firearm, or any type of striking weapon, out of fear of injuring my fellow officer.*

Notes: This scenario is specifically designed to see if you are the type of person who thinks of going to your "tools of the trade" first. A reality of law enforcement is that there are times when the only option is to engage in hand-to-hand combat with a suspect. This scenario leaves no room to use a firearm, baton, pepper spray, or even a Taser®, due to the close proximity of the other officer.

Use of Force – Scenario #3

Scenario: You are dispatched to a call of an Assault in progress.   When you arrive at the scene, you see a male standing over a female on the ground with a hammer in his hand. You then witness the male suspect strike the female victim in the head with the hammer. As you enter the building, you are approximately 45 feet away from the suspect and see him raise the hammer for another strike to the victim. How would you respond?

Sample answer: *I would be obligated to respond with deadly force in this situation. The suspect has already proven that he is attempting to injure or kill the victim with a hammer strike to the head, and another strike to the head could be deadly. My primary duty as a law enforcement officer is to protect the citizens. I am authorized to use deadly force to protect my life or the life of others, so the victim's safety is paramount. The distance is fifteen yards, and I believe that this is an acceptable distance from which to discharge my firearm. Once I stopped the threat from the suspect, I would call for medical help for the victim and then notify the dispatcher, and my supervisors, that a shooting has taken place.*

Notes: This scenario is there to see if you are willing to speak out loud what needs to be done.   Too often, candidates think that they need to "talk a suspect down" or use some other type of device to disarm a suspect. This is not always the case. Your job as a police officer will bring you in contact with some people who have no respect for human life, or the law.   If that person puts you in a situation in which you have to use deadly force to protect an innocent third party, be confident in your decision to take that action.

Ethics – Scenario #4

Scenario: You and your partner are on patrol and have just arrested a suspect. While placing the handcuffed suspect in the back of the patrol car, the suspect turns and spits on your partner. You then witness your partner strike the handcuffed suspect in the face several times with his closed fists. What would you do in this situation?

Sample answer: *This is an unfortunate situation in that there is only one clear-cut answer. I would notify my supervisor as to what had taken place and what I personally observed. The actions taken by my fellow officer were out of line and not representative of my police agency. I believe that not reporting this action would endanger the integrity of the police department, as well as the careers of all the officers involved in the arrest. I would assist in any investigation conducted by my agency or any other that takes place.*

Notes: This is a tough scenario. The law enforcement world is a tight one, and one in which you have to trust the other officers around you. In reality, this scenario is the type of incident that ends up with ten officers fired because they were trying to protect one. All law enforcement officers are held to a higher standard and that professionalism is what's required in this case. This is a straight forward ethics check, do not let any thoughts of "the blue line" or "wall of silence" enter your mind when answering this question. Believe me, if you are going before an oral board, this type of scenario WIL

Decision Making – Scenario #5

Scenario: You are on foot patrol and witness a person crouching down near a homeless person who is sleeping on a bench. You observe that the person is taking belongings from the pockets of the sleeping homeless person's jacket, and from the sleeping homeless person's bag. How would you handle this situation?

Sample answer: *I would immediately detain the person taking the items from the sleeping homeless person. Just because a person is homeless and sleeping on a bench does not mean that they deserve to be victimized. After detaining the suspect, I would wake the sleeping homeless man and ask him if the suspect had his permission or consent to take his property. If the homeless man informed me that the suspect did not have consent, and that he wished to pursue charges, I would then work the arrest like any other. Once I received the information for the criminal complaint, I would ask the homeless person if they need any assistance in finding a place to sleep in hopes to reduce the risk of further victimization.*

Notes: As stated in the answer above, it is very important that you, the candidate, extend victims rights to all people. Along with the criminal aspect of this scenario, make sure to address the social aspect of a person sleeping on a bench. Is there something you can do to help, even for the night? Don't forget the little things in these types of sc

Ethics – Scenario #6

Scenario: You are on patrol and witness a car weaving down the road. As you prepare to make a traffic stop, you witness the vehicle strike a concrete barrier and come to a stop. When you approach the driver's side door of the vehicle, you smell a strong odor of alcohol. As the driver steps out of his vehicle, you recognize him as a Captain on your police department. The Captain informs you who he is and yells at you to let him go. How would you handle this investigation?

Sample answer: *While I would show the proper respect to the person who holds the rank of Captain in my police department, I would also have no choice but to conduct a full investigation into the incident. I would conduct field sobriety tests on the Captain and advise him that I was conducting a Driving While Intoxicated investigation. I would then run the investigation as if the Captain was any other citizen. Departmentally, I would contact my supervisor and advise him about the investigation taking place. I would ask my supervisor if there were any other steps that I needed to take to meet departmental guidelines for this situation. If the Captain were to be taken into custody, I would do my best to make sure that any police department property was removed from the vehicle and turned over to my supervisor for safe keeping. I would then complete my criminal investigation.*

Notes: Another tough situation, no one like's the thought of having to arrest another officer. Hopefully, when you become a police officer, it's something that you never have to do. Again, the actions of one officer, in this case the Captain, could endanger the department and your career if not handled correctly. The board is trying to determine if you will turn a blind eye to a crime if the suspect is another police officer. Remember that the board will most likely be made up of civilians as well as classified officers. They do not want to hear that different rules apply to people that are wearing the badge.

Decision-Making – Scenario #7

Scenario: You are dispatched to a call of a sexual assault that just occurred. When you arrive at the call, you recognize the victim as a known prostitute whom you have personally arrested several times. The prostitute tells you that she did agree to have sex for money with a "john", but begged him to stop when he became violent with her. The prostitute claims that the "john" beat her, sexually assaulted her, and then fled the scene. There are signs of physical abuse on the prostitute's face. How would you handle this situation?

Sample answer: *I would handle this case no differently than any other sexual assault call I was dispatched to. While I understand that there was initially an agreement between the victim and the suspect, that agreement was terminated when the victim told the suspect to stop. I would make sure the victim received all the proper medical attention that she needed, as well as follow whatever procedures required to gather evidence for the criminal investigation. I would reassure the victim that even though I had arrested her before, that I would do everything I could to make sure her attacker was caught and charged for this crime.*

Notes: Obviously this scenario deals with victim's rights and decision-making. Can you separate your feelings for a person whom you have personally arrested over and over and realize that today, that person is your victim? Take a straight path on this type of scenario. Anybody, anytime, can become a victim. The prostitution angle does not matter in this particular scenario; the end result is the same. You are dealing with a victim who needs to be afforded all the rights that she is due.

Public interaction – Scenario #8

Scenario: You are on patrol and witness a slow moving vehicle hit a parked car, run a stop sign and almost hit two pedestrians in the crosswalk. As you attempt to conduct the traffic stop you see the car is swerving in the roadway and moving extremely slow. When the car comes to a stop and you make contact with the driver, you observe that he is an 85 year old male. How would you handle this situation?

Sample answer: *The first thing that I would do is to try and determine if there is a medical issue with this driver. Due to the advanced age of the driver, there are issues such as Alzheimer's disease and dementia that could be playing a role in this incident. If the driver were completely aware of his actions, and showed no signs of medical issues, I would conduct a standard hit and run investigation. However, if signs of medical issues were present, I would contact the appropriate medical personnel for assistance. I would attempt to contact the driver's family to assist in this situation. I would stay with this driver until he was either transported to a medical facility or retrieved by family members so that I could ensure he was safe when he left the scene. I would then attempt to find the driver/owner of the parked vehicle that was struck and make sure he was aware of the incident, as well as provide him with the necessary insurance information and police report number.*

Notes: This type of scenario involves decision-making and compassion. The board is trying to determine if you are the type of person who is quick to arrest someone without exploring other options, or fully investigating the circumstances. Did the driver commit a hit and run in this scenario? Yes, he did. Was there any criminal intent behind his actions? No, there was not. There are plenty of people out there who are knowingly and willingly committing crimes. The board will try to determine if you know the difference between the driver in this scenario and one of those people who clearly have criminal intent.

Decision-making – Scenario #9

Scenario: You are assigned to day shift patrol, which starts at 0400 in the morning. One of your fellow officers has started to come in to work, load up his patrol car, and then find a place to go to sleep for a couple of hours. You have observed him sleeping on duty on more than one occasion. How would you handle this?

Sample answer: *I would speak to my fellow officer one on one. I would explain to him that while he sleeps, the rest of us are out there running calls and picking up his slack. I would ask him if there are any issues outside of work that are causing him to be so tired when he comes in. If there is something outside of work that is causing him to be so tired, it could affect his performance and his safety. I would make it clear to him that the other officers are counting on him to stay awake and pull his weight in the patrol area.*

Notes: This scenario is there to let you know that you are not expected to go to your supervisor for every personnel issue. This is a minor issue between coworkers. There is no crime being committed, no civil rights being violated, or any other extreme issue to deal with. Nobody likes a lazy coworker, and a supervisor may have to intervene at some point, but do not be afraid to show the initiative and address the issue yourself.

Ethics – Scenario #10

Scenario: You and your partner respond to a Burglary call at a convenience store. You have secured the building and are leaving the scene. When you return to the patrol car, your partner offers you a candy bar that he has just taken from the store. You notice that he has taken several small items from the store without paying. When you ask him about the items, he responds "Don't worry, they'll think the burglars took that stuff." What action would you take in this scenario and why?

Sample answer: *I feel that I would have no choice but to report my partner to my supervisor in this instance. While I realize that the dollar amount of a few candy bars is most likely minimal, it's the mindset shown by my fellow officer that would concern me the most. As police officers we are expected to catch the criminals who commit crimes against the citizens, not take part in the crime itself. If my partner is of the belief that he can commit a crime due to his position as a police officer, in my opinion, this is not a person that needs to wear the same badge I do.*

Notes: This is another straightforward ethics scenario. There is no gray area here. You witnessed another police officer commit a theft from a scene, so it needs to be reported. It has been my experience that the officers who think the law does not apply to them always start small. If someone has that mindset, they may progress to shaking people down on traffic stops, or stealing money from a warrant scene. Don't stray here, always give the ethical answer.

Use of Force - Scenario #11

Scenario: You are dispatched to a call concerning a female who is acting erratically and is threatening violence towards her family members. When you arrive, you observe a female who is screaming and appears to be out of touch with reality. Her family members advise you that she has not taken her medication in days and is having a psychotic episode. The female does not have any weapons. What would you do in this situation?

Sample answer: *I would begin by asking the family a few questions to learn the female's name and current medical condition. I would then try to talk to the female and calm the situation. If the female did not respond to voice commands, I would attempt to restrain the female for her safety and that of her family. I would attempt this restraint maneuver with the absolute minimal amount of force necessary. Once I was able to get the female restrained, I would contact the dispatcher and ask for an ambulance to make the scene and verify that the female has no other medical conditions that need to be addressed. If she were clear of further medical issues, I would take the female to a facility designed to help psychiatric patients and place her in a safe situation.*

Notes: This type of question is there to find out if you can tell the difference between the various use of force situations. Do you want to be the Officer who has the entire family turn on you because you were too heavy-handed and showed no compassion? Do you want to deal with the lawsuits or complaints that would inevitably follow a heavy-handed response to this type of scene? Believe me, you do not want to be that Officer. As an Officer, you will be expected to know how to use force, but show compassion at the same time. It is important in this type of scenario to display your sympathy for the family for having to see their daughter in this condition. You need to present yourself as the compassionate, caring police officer.

Decision Making – Scenario #12

Scenario: You are on patrol and conduct a traffic stop. As you approach the car, the driver rolls down his window and screams at you that he is best of friends with the Mayor of your city. How would you handle this situation? What if you approach the car and the person driving is your mother in law? Does this change the situation?

Sample answer: *I would continue with my traffic investigation like any other stop. Anyone can claim to be friends, or relatives, of politicians or people that they feel may sway my decision-making. I would gather the information and, if the situation warranted, issue the citation. As for my mother in law, I would never issue a citation to my mother in law for a minor traffic violation. My authority as a police officer grants me discretion as to when, and to whom, I write a citation. The long-term effects of writing my mother in law a citation are not worth any amount of money to the city.*

Notes: This scenario is all about discretion. Anybody can claim to be best friends with the mayor, chief, whoever, doesn't really matter. It's up to you whether or not you issue the citation. So be clear that you would check the situation out and then make the determination as to whether or not you write the citation. Concerning the mother in law issue, oral boards are trying to determine what kind of person you are when you sit down and answer these questions. Are you really the type of person that would write your mother in law a traffic ticket when you didn't have to? Are you the type of person that cannot see the negative effects that this action would have? Or are you the type of person that is so badge heavy that you believe "no one is above the law?" Use some common sense; police departments are not looking for robots that cannot make a smart decision. Writing a ticket to your mother in law is definitely not a smart decision.

Use of Force – Scenario #13

Scenario: You are arriving at the Municipal courthouse for traffic court and you are in full uniform. You see a male get out of his vehicle with an assault rifle in his hand and start moving towards the courthouse. What action would you take? What if you see the shooter enter the building and you are by yourself?

Sample answer: *I would immediately notify dispatch that there is an "active shooter" situation at the courthouse and to send backup as soon as possible. I would then move towards the shooter and attempt to place myself in a position to confront the threat. If the shooter moves out of my sight, I would wait for the first backup units to arrive and immediately begin to clear the building until we find and deal with the threat. If I could maintain sight of the shooter, I would take action to deal with the threat, either through verbal commands, or if necessary, deadly force. I feel that if I ran into a building by myself, without knowing the shooters location, this could possibly give the shooter an opportunity to ambush me, and therefore provide him with another weapon and ammunition.*

Notes: Unfortunately, the "active shooter" scenario is becoming an extremely important part of police training and mindset. Gone are the days of surrounding a building and waiting for SWAT to arrive. If you have a person with a gun inside a building, every officer is expected to confront the shooter before they can harm any civilians. This action is best undertaken with a team of officers so that all angles are covered. This depends, of course, on whether or not you know where the shooter is, and what the tactical situation is. What the board wants to know here is whether or not you are willing to pursue an active shooter and deal with the threat.

Decision-Making – Scenario #14

Scenario: You are dispatched to a minor accident with no injuries. While on the way to that call, you hear a call about a "person down" that you are two blocks away from. Which call would you respond to and why?

Sample answer: *I would respond to the "person down" call since life takes priority over property. I would be obligated to check the "person down" call and see if the person is in need of medical attention, or possibly the victim of a crime. The accident, since there are no injuries, is something that can wait until the person's well being can be determined.*

Notes: This is pretty basic; life will always take priority over property. Let the board know that, even though an accident investigation is important, it is secondary to the well being of a citizen. This will let them know that you have your priorities in place. You do not want the board to believe that you would place a higher value on a damaged vehicle than the safety of the citizens.

Ethics and Integrity – Scenario #15

Scenario: You are working patrol overtime and notice that other officers have turned in overtime slips, but did not work the shift. When you inquire about it, you are told that you can get in on the "scam" if you keep quiet about it. How would you respond to this situation and why?

Sample answer: *I would be obligated to immediately report this situation to my supervisor. What these other officers are doing is theft and is a crime. I would not endanger my career, or my freedom, for the few dollars that an overtime shift is going to bring in. I would also be obligated to cooperate in any investigation that resulted from this situation. There is no justification for what these officers are doing, so I would not allow anyone to make me feel that I am not a team player.*

Notes: I understand that nobody wants to be a "snitch," but if you were built for prison, would you be trying to be Police Officer? Police work is a long road that can be sometimes rewarding, and often trying. Do you really need your fellow officers placing you in a situation that could land you in jail? Once they do that, they've crossed the line and are no longer your brothers and sisters in blue. Do not hesitate to do the right thing here. This scenario only has one correct answer!

Ethics and Integrity – Scenario #16

Scenario: You are on patrol and respond to a call concerning domestic violence. When you arrive on the scene, you recognize the female, who has obvious signs of assault, as the wife of another officer at your station. How would you handle this situation?

Sample answer: *I would have to investigate this case like any other domestic violence case. The fact that the possible suspect is a police officer can have no bearing on how the criminal investigation is conducted. I would notify my supervisor that the possible suspect is a police officer so that he may take the proper departmental action. I would make sure that the victim is checked out medically, and made aware of all the services that are available to victims of domestic violence. I would then complete whatever level of investigation into the incident that my job description allowed me to.*

Notes: These kinds of questions often trip up a candidate. The board is trying to determine if you would give a police officer suspect special treatment. You need to be very clear that a police officer suspect is just another suspect in this case. You are telling your supervisor so that he/she can handle the administrative end of things. You need to assure the board that domestic violence can never be tolerated, no matter who the suspect is.

Decision-Making – Scenario #17

Scenario: You are dispatched to a call concerning a possible drunk driver. You find the vehicle and are able to get it pulled over. When you approach the vehicle, the female driver is extremely intoxicated and combative. Upon further inspection, you notice a small toddler in the back seat, strapped in a seatbelt, but not in a car seat. What actions would you take in this scenario?

Sample answer: *I would begin by attempting to calm the female suspect down and get some information on the child.   I would also immediately call for backup to help with the child while I conducted the Driving while Intoxicated field investigation.   If I decide to arrest the driver, which seems likely if she's intoxicated, I would make sure the child was picked up by either a family member or social services.   I would then attempt to get charges on the female for not only DWI, but Endangering a Child as well.   I would make sure that my paperwork referenced the placement of the child in the vehicle and also make sure that social services conducted their own follow up to this incident.*

Notes: This scenario wants to make sure that you understand that there can be multiple levels to a situation. Are you so locked into the DWI that you forget about the child endangerment? Are you going to attempt a follow up with social services to check on the child?   The board wants to know that you can think outside of the box in these situations, and will not get tunnel vision when conducting an investigation.

Use of Force – Scenario #18

Scenario: You are dispatched to a call concerning loud noise, possibly fireworks, coming from a field behind some homes. As you drive up to the area you hear a loud pop. You approach the area on foot and see a 10-year-old boy with a rifle in his hands approaching you from the field area. What would you do in this situation?

Sample answer: *I would immediately look for cover before I even make verbal contact with the young boy. I would not want to scare him and make him do something rash with the rifle. I would then advise him, in a calm voice, that he needs to put the rifle down so that we can talk. His response will give me a better idea as to what I'm dealing with. I would have my weapon out of the holster, but not in view, while I'm trying to determine the facts of the incident. Once the rifle is on the ground, if that's how the scenario develops, I would have the boy step away from it so I could make it safe. I would then secure the rifle and find the boy's parents. I would advise them what happened and discuss any possible criminal violations.*

Notes: The board wants to know if you're a trigger-happy person with this question. As a police officer you will have the greater responsibility to diffuse the situation and make sure that no one gets hurt, even though there are guns involved. Does the fact that someone has a weapon in their hands mean that you should shoot them immediately? This scenario shows you that this is not always the case. It is important that you relate to the board that you will be tactically proficient while, at the same time, keeping the situation from getting out of hand with a heavy handed response.

Use of Force – Scenario #19

Scenario: You are dispatched to a shooting in progress at a junior high school. You arrive on scene and are told of a 12-year-old boy who has a gun and is in the cafeteria. When you run to the cafeteria, you see the 12 year old actively shooting at other students. What would you do in this situation?

Sample answer: *I would have to immediately use deadly force to eliminate the threat. I have seen the suspect actively engaged in shooting at innocent third parties. I would be duty bound to engage that suspect and make him stop shooting at all costs.*

Notes: This situation is cut and dry, the suspect is an active shooter and needs to be engaged until he stops shooting. The board will throw his age out there in an attempt to get you to hesitate. The suspect's actions determine your actions in this scenario. Do not let the board place doubt in your mind due to the suspect's age.

Suggestions

Here are a few things that I have observed during my own interviews, and from the other candidates that were there with me. These observations should be taken as just that, observations/suggestions, but remember that I have twenty years worth of interviewing for assignments, promotions, and now, new agencies under my belt.

1. Wear a suit/pant suit – It's very important that the board knows that you are placing the proper importance on your interview. If you go into the interview looking sloppy, or dressed too casual, it will immediately give the board a negative impression. If you are a lateral officer, it is NOT ok to wear your police uniform to an oral board interview with another agency.

2. Make sure your hair is trim and neat – Remember that when you walk into that interview room, the board is immediately looking at you as a potential representative of their agency. You do not want to show a lack of respect to the board by looking anything less than your best. Again, appearance is very important, the board WILL take it into consideration.

3. Do not go into the interview with a hardline stance on every situation. Modern day policing requires dealing with people on all levels, and being able to react quickly to changing situations. Let the board know that you are an open-minded person who is willing to view every call for what it is and not make any prejudgments. The board is

not concerned about how tough you are, they are concerned about the agency being sued if they hire the wrong person.

4. Most importantly, just relax and listen. When the board asks you a question, pause a beat; show them that you are thinking about the scenario. The scenarios are very rarely timed; so don't feel rushed into giving a bad answer. It will carry much more weight if you take the time to form your answer and give a decisive, thoughtful response to the scenario.

Final Notes

I could go on and on with different variations of the same scenarios, but they all boil down to the same thing. Are you the type of person that the hiring agency can trust with the power and authority that comes with being a certified police officer? This is the only thing the board is trying to determine.

The oral boards are often made up of a combination of police officers and citizens that either work for the agency, or are part of citizens groups that work with/monitor the police department. It is this very reason why you, as the candidate, must maintain your composure at all times during the interview. While a veteran officer may be able to decipher some hard line answer you give to a question, the citizen will only envision a power mad individual with a gun in their fair city.

Modern day police work has changed on many levels. However, the backbone of the business has not. You, as a police officer, will be expected to deal with high stress, and often dangerous, situations. However, you are expected to keep calm, cool and collected while you are dealing with these situations. It is not an easy thing to do, but it is required if you want to have a long, successful career. If you're reading this book, the desire to do the work is already there. Keep your head on a swivel and enjoy the job.